W9-CKF-802

FEB   2008   WITHDRAWN

INDIAN TRAILS
PUBLIC LIBRARY DISTRICT
WHEELING, ILLINOIS 60090
847-459-4100
www.indiantrailslibrary.org

Food Groups

Oils

PROPERTY OF INDIAN TRAILS
PUBLIC LIBRARY DISTRICT

Lola Schaefer

Heinemann Library
Chicago, Illinois

© 2008 Heinemann Library
a division of Reed Elsevier Inc.
Chicago, Illinois

Customer Service 888-454-2279
Visit our website at www.heinemannraintree.com

All rights reserved. No part of this publication may be reproduced or transmitted in any form or by any means, electronic or mechanical, including photocopying, recording, taping, or any information storage and retrieval system, without permission in writing from the publisher.

Designed by Joanna Hinton-Malivoire
Printed and bound in China by South China Printing Co. Ltd.

12 11 10 09 08
10 9 8 7 6 5 4 3 2 1

ISBN-10: 1-4329-0144-3 (hc) -- ISBN-10: 1-4329-0151-6

Library of Congress Cataloging-in-Publication Data
Schaefer, Lola M., 1950-
Oils / Lola M. Schaefer.
p. cm. -- (Food groups)
Includes bibliographical references and index.
ISBN 978-1-4329-0144-8 (hc) -- ISBN 978-1-4329-0151-6 (pb) 1. Lipids in human nutrition--Juvenile literature. 2. Vegetable oils in human nutrition--Juvenile literature. I. Title.
QP751.S19 2008
612.3'97--dc22

2007008974

Acknowledgements
The publishers would like to thank the following for permission to reproduce photographs: © Alamy p. **15** (MedioImages); © Brand X Pictures p. **14**; © Copix p. **7**; © Corbis p. **8** (Tim Pannell); © Getty Images p. **9** (Photolibrary); © Harcourt Education Ltd pp. **4** (Tudor Photography), **6** (Tudor Photography), **10** (Tudor Photography), **11** (Tudor Photography), **3** (Tudor Photography), **16** (Tudor Photography), **19** (Tudor Photography), **24** (Tudor Photography), **25** (Tudor Photography), **26** (Tudor Photography), **27** (Tudor Photography); © PhotoEdit Inc. p. **17** (David Young-Wolff); Photolibrary pp. **12** (Anthony Blake), **20** (Anthony Blake), **21** (Foodpix), **22** (Anthony Blake), **23** (Photononstop), **29** (Bsip); © Punchstock p. **28**; USDA Center for Nutrition Policy and Promotion p. **5**.

Cover photograph reproduced with permission © Getty Images (StockFood Creative).

Every effort has been made to contact copyright holders of any material reproduced in this book. Any omissions will be rectified in subsequent printings if notice is given to the publishers.

Disclaimer
All Internet addresses (URLs) given in this book were valid at the time of going to press. However, due to the dynamic nature of the Internet, some addresses may have changed or ceased to exist since publication. While the author and the publishers regret any inconvenience this may cause readers, no responsibility for any such changes can be accepted by either the author or the publishers.

Contents

Some words are shown in bold, **like this**. You can find out what they mean by looking in the glossary.

What Are Oils?

Oils are **fats** that are **liquids** at room temperature. Healthy oils have few **trans fats** and are good for your body. People all over the world eat oils in foods.

The oils in salmon are very good for the body.

The body needs oils as well as food from the five **food groups**. You need a little oil each day as part of a good **diet**. Oils help your body work well and stay healthy.

Where Oils Come From

Oils are found inside some fish. They are also inside seeds, nuts, and plants. If you eat an ear of corn, you are eating corn oil.

Healthy oils are found inside many foods.

Peanuts are pressed to make oil that can be used in cooking.

People make oils. They press or squeeze plants and use the oil that comes from the leaves or seeds. Walnut oil comes from pressed walnuts.

Adding Oils to Foods

Bakers add oils to breads, cakes, or muffins to make these foods moist. Some dry foods would not taste good without oils. They would also be hard to swallow.

Many bakers use natural vegetable oils because they are healthier.

Extra virgin olive oil is the healthiest oil.

Cooks add oils to pasta or rice. The oils keep **grains** from sticking together. Oils also make foods like sauces or salads taste better.

What Oils Look Like

Oils are thick **liquids**. You can see through oils because they are clear or almost clear. Most oils are stored in bottles.

Many people cook foods in corn oil.

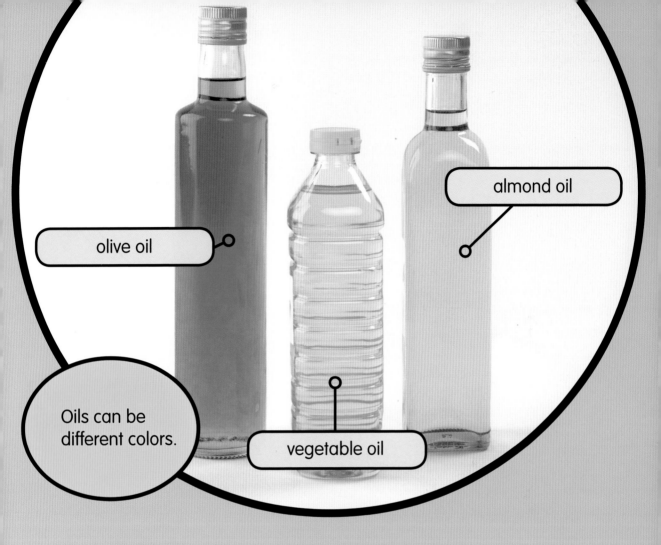

olive oil

almond oil

Oils can be different colors.

vegetable oil

Most oils have some color. Olive oil has a light green color. Corn oil is light yellow. When you mix oil into a food, you cannot see the oil.

How Oils Taste

You would not enjoy eating an oil by itself. Oils have little flavor of their own. They take on or add flavor to the spices or foods that they touch.

These vegetables are being cooked in sesame oil.

Dipping oil for bread

Please ask an adult to help you.

- Mix all the ingredients together in a small bowl.
- Let the mixture sit for one hour.
- Serve and enjoy with warm bread.

You will need:
- 6 tablespoons (tbsp) of olive oil
- ½ tbsp of chopped basil or parsley
- 1 crushed garlic clove
- a pinch of salt and red pepper flakes

Serve bread and dipping oil with a large salad for a healthy meal.

13

Why We Need to Eat Oils

Oils help keep your body healthy. They have **vitamin** E. This vitamin helps protect the **cells** in your body and fights some **diseases**.

Oils from plants, fish, and seeds give you energy to work and play.

Oils help keep
your skin healthy.

Oils protect your bones and keep your
skin smooth and strong. Some oils are
good for your brain. Some oils help keep
you warm and help you grow.

How Many Oils Do You Need?

Most children 5–10 years old need 4–5 teaspoons of oil every day. It is best to eat these oils in healthy nuts, fish, and seeds. Or you can add olive oil to your food.

Cod is a white fish. Eating fish is one good way to eat healthy oils.

You can get some of the oil that your body needs by eating peanuts.

Your body only needs a little oil each day. If you eat too much oil, your body will not work well and you could feel ill. You could also put on extra weight.

Oils to Eat for Breakfast

If you eat pancakes or waffles for breakfast, you will be eating oil. These foods have oil in them. The oil helps the food to cook and makes it taste good.

Only add a little oil to your food.

Peanut butter is a good source of healthy oil, **protein**, and **fiber**.

Some people spread peanut butter over a **whole wheat** bagel or toast. Plus, some people add walnuts or pecans to their cereal. Good oils are inside all of these nuts.

Oils to Eat for Lunch

At lunchtime, you might eat some pasta mixed with olive oil and cheese. Or you might lightly cook some onions in vegetable oil. Add vegetable broth and make onion soup.

It only takes a little oil to cook these onions for soup.

One avocado can make two of these tasty sandwiches.

An avocado has healthy oil in it. You can slice an avocado and put it on **whole wheat** bread. Add cucumber and lettuce to make a healthy sandwich.

Oils to Eat for Dinner

For dinner, you can eat a stir-fried mixture of vegetables in some peanut oil. Add some soy sauce. Serve the cooked vegetables over brown rice.

This colorful mixture of vegetables has been cooked in oil.

Olive oil and vinegar salad dressing

Please ask an adult to help you.

- Mix all the ingredients together in a small bowl.
- Serve over a mixed salad, and enjoy.

You will need:
- 3 tablespoons (tbsp) of balsamic vinegar
- 6 tbsp of extra virgin olive oil
- ½ teaspoon of crushed garlic
- a pinch of thyme, basil, oregano, and pepper

Oils to Eat for Snacks

Seeds and nuts contain healthy oils and make great snacks. Mix a handful of sunflower seeds, almonds, walnuts, and pumpkin seeds together. This makes a healthy snack.

Store this mix in a sealed container in a cool place.

This snack will give you a boost of energy.

Peanut butter tastes good at snack time. Try spreading it on celery, apples, **whole wheat** crackers, or breadsticks.

Keeping Oils Fresh

Store oils in a bottle or container with a tight lid. It is best to keep oils in a cool, dark cabinet. If you live somewhere that gets hot, keep your oils and seeds in the refrigerator.

Oils that are sealed and stored in a cabinet will last much longer than those left out in the sun and heat.

Never eat an oil that has a bad smell or taste.

Oils do not like light, heat, or fresh air. If they are placed in a warm or well-lit space, they might **spoil**. The oil would then have a bad smell and taste.

Do Oils Alone Keep You Healthy?

Oils alone cannot keep you healthy. You need a **diet** of many good foods. Eat from each **food group** every day and drink three or four glasses of water.

Exercising with friends can be a lot of fun.

Sleep helps your body rest and rebuild.

As well as eating healthy foods, your body needs regular **exercise**. You should try to get a little each day. You also need to get plenty of sleep each night. Sleep helps you stay strong and well.

Glossary

cell smallest part of a living thing

diet what a person usually eats and drinks

disease illness that keeps a person from normal day-to-day activities

exercise physical activity that helps keep a body healthy and fit

fat nutrient in food that gives the body energy. The body only needs a little fat each day.

fiber rough part of food that is not digested. Fiber helps carry food through the body.

food group foods that have the same kind of nutrients. There are five main food groups, plus oils.

grains foods such as wheat, rye, oats, rice, and corn

liquid substance that can flow or be poured

protein nutrient in food that gives the body energy and helps it grow

spoil when a food becomes too old and is no longer safe to eat

trans fat a kind of fat that is unhealthy for the body

vitamin nutrient in food that the body needs to stay healthy. Nutrients help the body work correctly.

whole wheat made from flour that uses whole grains of wheat

Find Out More

Books to read

Miller, Edward. *The Monster Health Book: A Guide to Eating Healthy, Being Active and Feeling Great for Monsters and Kids*. New York: Holiday House, 2006.

Nelson, Robin. *Fats, Oils, Sweets*. Minneapolis, MN: Lerner, Chelsea Clubhouse Food, 2003.

Parenzan, Carol. *Fats, Oils and Sweets*. New York: Scholastic, 2006.

Websites to visit

KidsHealth: The Food Guide Pyramid
http://www.kidshealth.org/kid/stay_healthy/food/pyramid.html

United States Department of Agriculture:
Inside the Pyramid – Oils
http://www.mypyramid.gov/pyramid/oils.html

Index

3 1125 00718 6578